# JOURNEY TO SUNRISE

Tuyet Beatty-Moore

*Trafford rev. 01/04/2013*

 www.trafford.com

North America & international
toll-free: 1 888 232 4444 (USA & Canada)
phone: 250 383 6864 ♦ fax: 812 355 4082

This book is dedicated to my husband, children, and parents. Who I love and thank God for blessing me to be apart of your lives daily.

I also dedicate this book to my grandmothers; Lilley "Verna" Windley, Lossie Belle Beatty, and Ellen Turner. Who gave of their time everyday for a year helping to care for me and my children. Their great grandchildren. I love you.

# Acknowledgements

To my husband and children who encouraged me to finish the project.

To my parents for believing in the project and your endless prayers.

Thank you to my friends that supported me in helping with the many hours proof reading, sharing lots of great ideas, encouragement and prayers.

To God I give all the glory and praise!

# CONTENTS

# Introduction

As one of the many passages of faith God preordained in my life, Journey to Sunrise is a witness of conviction and gratefulness of a Preachers Kid (P.K.) as to the grace and mercy of Christ Jesus. This is a chronological account of how Christ Jesus answered prayers from my heart and prayers prayed intellectually. I had not yet become aware of how God and Christ Jesus had been working in my life from the age of twenty four, when I was diagnosed with Multiple Sclerosis at which time I lost my eyesight for three months (up to the point of yet another miraculous life altering event years later.) This event caused me to stay in a constant prayerful relationship with Christ Jesus more than ever before. It caused me to build not only a stronger prayer life, but also more humbling and willfully trusting relationship with God the Father and Christ Jesus. Okay you're probably thinking aren't they the same? Let's see! As God tells us in His word, there is but one God, non-else. Isaiah 45:18, James 2:19, Revelations 1:8 just to reference a few of His scriptures. He is God the Father to all and over all. Alpha, the beginning, the creator of all things and Omega the end. God the Son our living example, Savior, Intercessor, and Comforter. And God the Holy Spirit our ever present help, our guide into all truth (John 16:13.) Each one is distinct and equally necessary and are one as God is omnipresent in our lives at all times (Hebrew 13:5).

This was a passage that was a blessing for and to me. Growing deeper into a more humbled, willful, genuine heart desiring an even greater presence of God the Father, my creator; God the Son, Christ Jesus my Savior and intercessor; and God the Holy Spirit my ever present help. It was a daily blessing God pre-ordained for my family and friends chosen to be with me giving me support and receiving the blessing of encouragement that He had waiting for us all during this critical season in my life. Others were blessed that Christ Jesus allowed to cross my path during that time of anointed rehabilitation of the body and mind, and are being blessed even today. To God be all the glory! It is my hope that you will be encouraged by this witness and scriptures that God allowed the Holy Spirit to give me then and now.

# Heavenly Concierge

We all have prepared ourselves to take a trip and in preparing ourselves for this much anticipated trip we first begin by making a mental list of what we're going to need to take, what we'd like to take, and what we'll actually have room to take depending on our luggage and who we're traveling with and how we're traveling. Whether it is by car, plane, train, bus, or a varied combination. We also take the time to think about the length of our trip, how much money we have budgeted to spend, research the weather and what it's' going to be like as we travel and while we're at our destination.

Preparation is the key. When we've planned well, packed all the essentials that we know we'll be needing and throw in a couple extra's for those "JUST IN CASE" moments, then we smile and pat ourselves on the back because we did a great job preparing so the trip will be a success.

The same time, planning and preparation is what God does for the predestined journeys in our lives. I know this now and God keeps me ever mindful of His omnipresence and His merciful power of deliverance and healing in my life. I look back over the years of my life, as we all do, but most of the time we have tunnel vision. Not seeing God's blessings, grace and mercies over our lives. *Tunnel vision? Yes, we are so focused on our intended agenda of passage, we are peripherally blinded. And with that same intent we focus on the voyage of life ahead of us without our ears opened to hear Him speaking to us "TRUST*

*ME, TRUST ME, I PACKED YOU FOR THE JOURNEY.*" But God in all His glory blessed me to see His blessings of grace, mercy, healing and deliverance in my life when there was and is no explanation for the physical ailments that plagued my body without warning from my young adult years through my adult years. I was in the prime of life, successful career, wife and mother of a beautiful baby girl and soon to be mother to that much desired baby boy. My life was wonderful, it was all that I wanted it to be. God had answered my prayers and blessed me with a great husband, children, abundant finances, as far as I was concerned, I had the beautiful fragrant rose pedals of life, my life was a bed of roses. I had forgotten about the thorns of the rose, "Ouch!"

On January 3, 2002, God answered a prayer that I whispered on the third Sunday of June in the summer of 2001. He blessed me to hear His Holy Spirit speaking in a whisper of comfort, "Trust Me, call on the name of Christ Jesus." Not understanding why God had enlightened and blessed my spirit with this word, confused, I did just as God had instructed out of obedience. Not just one time but many times throughout each night for seven months, I awakened to here myself calling on the name of Jesus.

My journey of willful obedience began on that third Sunday morning in June 2001 at church around testimony time; see my father is the Pastor of the church that my family and I are members of. Yes I'm a PK *(Preacher's Kid)* Oh you thought that made life easier! Not by a long shot! My father has been a Pastor for twenty plus years therefore I grew up in the church and I . . . . as it seems it should be, naturally I serve in the ministry. I'm the Minister of Music, so you know that I would know better than to mock anyone that stood to testify as to the goodness of God in their life. But I had developed a habit of doing so when one of the church mothers would stand to testify each Sunday. I would look around the church and if

I saw a new face, I new that this particular Church Mother was going to stand and tell that same testimony. Because she'd shared her testimony every Sunday that there was someone new sitting in the congregation, that meant that the members heard it over and over again. So it became a habit each Sunday to mock her as she'd stand to testify of God's deliverance. The congregation couldn't see my face, because of the position of the keyboard; my back was turned to them. The Pastor couldn't see me because I was boxed in by the side podium, the only ones that had clear view of me was the choir members and they'd get a kick out of it every Sunday, facing the congregation trying not to laugh. And of course God saw me, who I new was not at all pleased with me. This particular Sunday was Father's Day. God has a way of encrypting His time, seasons of change, exodus from ourselves in both our hearts and memories. Testimony service had just ended and yes, Church Mother had given her usual testimony and I continued with my usual mocking. But this time was different, God disciplined me right on the spot! WHOOH! He allowed me to experience a spirit of sadness not for her, but for me. A sadness that I didn't have a heart-felt conviction of any kind toward God. I knew that I loved Him because if it were not for God and His son Jesus the Christ, I wouldn't be in existence, nor as successful as I was at that time in my life. But I didn't have that conviction that Church Mother had. An urgency of repentance for my actions toward her pressed on my heart. I immediately began to pray and asked God's forgiveness for what I had been doing every Sunday and had done that morning. I asked God to give me a conviction so that I could understand her loyalty and conviction to share her testimony with others. I to wanted to be a commissioned vessel that God would use to share the hope and over whelming love of Jesus the Christ with those whose paths I crossed.

At the conclusion of the service I went over to Church Mother, who sits on the second pew of the congregation behind me, and greeted her with a hug and warm smile and shared with her that I was glad to see her at service and assured her that the following Sunday I'd play her favorite praise song. She smiled and said in a soft voice, "Thank you, I'd like that!"

You know as we travel we all have land marks that become apart of our mental landscape and that day Church Mother became a part of mine. That Sunday was a big day for me, not just because it was Father's Day but it was also the day that my husband and I had chosen to share with my parents that I was pregnant with their second grandchild, but their first grandson. You see I didn't know how they were going to take it, not that they had any say in the matter, but I still cared how the news would affect them because our daughter was just twelve months old and I had just found out the week before Father's Day that I was five months pregnant with our son. This news was a wonderful gift for my husband, but at first it really threw me for a LOOP! Here I was walking around with a baby on my hip and pregnant again, my husband was overjoyed and didn't understand why I was having such a hard time accepting this pregnancy. I explained to him that this pregnancy was not in my plan, that's why I was taking those VERY, VERY expensive contraceptives that I took everyday as though my life depended on them. So that a mistake like that wouldn't happen, it just wasn't good financial planning. YOU KNOW KIDS ARE EXPENSIVE!! My husband then reminded me that NOTHING that GOD does is a mistake. I wouldn't have become pregnant regardless to the use of the contraceptives if it wasn't in God's plan; which by the way trumps my plan and yours. MY parents were surprised at the news but tickled with the idea of having two grands to spoil. The elation in their eyes served as a source of comfort for me, the anxious feeling began to ease. It's something about seeing the warm countenance of approval from your parents no matter how old you are. That is something that few are blessed to understand and realize the privilege of the endearing presence and wisdom of parents until their seasons have passed. Thank God that He blessed me with the understanding and endearing gratitude for the gift of parents that He planned just for me! As time progressed I realized how much I loved that little baby boy that grew inside of me and God had answered the prayer I prayed to be a wife to a husband that loved God and His way of life and a mother of both a boy and a girl. That was when God opened my eyes and heart to realize the true blessing of prayer and the belief in knowing that God hears and will answer in His ordained time.

As the weeks went by I waited in anticipation for the trial that I prayed for on that first Sunday in June. That trail that would convict me to testify as to God's goodness during the struggle to overcome that trial of circumstance. Watching and praying from day to day for this testimony to evolve in my daily routine God had begun to prepare me to go to the next level of my journey. While doing my weekly shopping in the Walmart Super Center I received a nudge from the Holy Spirit to go to the stationary isle. Instead I went to the book isle first to look for a book of daily devotions but I didn't find one, so then I went to the isle I was directed to go to first to look for paper so I thought, but God had another plan. On this isle completely out of place was a beautiful book that said, "Grant *me the serenity to accept the things that I can not change, courage to change the things I can, and the wisdom to know the difference. (Reinhold Niebuhr)* These were the words that I was searching for and didn't know it nor did I understand why those words gave me a sense of comfort for the feeling of urgency that I was experiencing. I then open the book expecting to see comforting religious poems and daily devotions only to find blank pages with a scripture at the top of every fifth page. I thought, now how can this help me? I've got to fill in the blanks! I put it in the cart, brought it home, and placed it on my night stand where it stayed for two and a half months or more before the Holy Spirit impressed upon my heart to write my prayers and thoughts in this journal. On Nov. 30, 2001 I began to write my prayers at the end of everyday and I did so until Jesus had me to journal my last prayer on the 22$^{nd}$ of December 2001 with a great feeling of peace and empowering comfort.

# The List

*Ephesians 6:1-24*

Not understanding the purpose, the Lord had me to place the journal on my night stand. I didn't know why, but I did so out of obedience having been raised to honor the authority and order of God and His word. The quote of encouragement on the cover of the journal became the second thing I said every morning after I thanked God for keeping and delivering me and my babies through yet another night. See there was something going on in my life at night that God speaks of in Ephesians 6:12, *we wrestle not against flesh and blood, but against principalities, against powers, against the rulers of the darkness of this world, against spiritual wickedness in high places.* I couldn't understand why God was allowing me to experience the spiritual warfare with Satan the ruler of darkness, during my pregnancy when I needed all the rest I could get.

Understanding and having been raised never to question God and remembering what my husband reminded me of, that God doesn't allow anything to happen that's not in HIS PLAN. It had begun to become very hard to over look the exhaustion that I was experiencing from my nightly battles with Satan. I awakened through out the night in a struggle, fighting to call on the name of Jesus, through Satan's persistent choking of my throat to keep me from calling the name of Jesus. I've awakened in a many a struggle not just feeling Satan choking me but also feeling Satan's grip on my wrist, feeling him holding me down asking me, "Where's your God now, see if you can call Jesus now!" I was awakened breathless screaming the name of Jesus every night! Each night I would pray to God to bless me with a peaceful sleep because I was so tired, I needed to rest. But it was as though God wasn't hearing me and my nightly struggle persisted with Satan until dawn. I continued to thank my God for his protection and deliverance of me and my babies because I strongly felt that it wasn't just me that was under attack: my children that God blessed were vulnerable to attack because I knew that Satan's urgency was to defeat me in the small fragment of time that God had allowed for him to test the strength of my faith, a time that seemed like would never end. You are probably wondering where my husband was during all of this? Sleeping like a baby. I would always ask my husband if he felt and heard my struggling and screaming during the night before and his answer was always, "No, why do you ask me this everyday?" I would always reply by saying, "I just don't want to disturb your rest." I thank God again for that because there was no need for the two of us to loose sleep. God showed me that even though we were married as one, what God has for me and my spiritual growth in my journey towards His kingdom takes a totally different route than that of my husband, but in the end through God's, will our individual journeys will take us to the same destination "THAT HOLY CITY, THE KINGDOM OF GOD!"

# Perfectly Packed

Ephesians 6:11-18


Now during this time I was in an avid search for some form of
dedication of our home back to God, I spoke with the Pastor in
regards to having the rededication of our home to God. It never
happened because the Pastor's schedule would not allow him
to come or someone in our home would be sick with a virus so
we would have to reschedule. I felt passionately that if I found
the perfect plaque, or cross to place in an area of our home that
it was meant to be in with prayer and anointing of our home
this would be a heart felt re-dedication of our home back to our
Lord and Savior Jesus the Christ. I never found anything but
on the first Sunday of Dec. of 2001 the choir members were
moved to show their appreciation for my service with the choir
by giving me individual gifts. In one of those gifts was a ceramic
antique cross with the fruits of the Holy Spirit carved in it and
there was a poem "All Things Will Work for Your Good." The
cross was perfect! And the poem was a quiet encouragement to
my soul. My husband and I walked through the house placing
it in the open spaces on each wall and the Holy Spirit led us to
the threshold of our bedroom door and that's where we placed
it. At that very moment I was blessed with a feeling of peace
and accomplishment. Still in my nightly wars I found that I
was not fearing or dreading my time of slumber but felt as
though each night God was blessing me to get stronger and
stronger in this nightly battle and the battles were becoming
shorter each night. As I journeyed through this time, the Holy

Spirit would bring back to memory the certain passages of verses from God's word that would cause me to research my bible on a daily basis. God placed within me a need to recall the entire scripture. God didn't just give me a need to recall but an overwhelming desire to know what He wanted me to hear in that scripture and how to apply it to my life instantly. God had placed a true urgency in my inner being, and my heart ached to understand why I had this sense of urgency. I knew that God was going to answer my prayers that He had me to write in my journal and the prayers that I whispered through out the hours and days of my season of spiritual and physical war with Satan ( *Ephesians 6:12*). I knew that God was going to will me a time of peaceful, rejuvenating sleep in His time. (Ephesians *6:10-11, "Be strong in the Lord and in the power of his might")*. I accepted this struggle of war; self implying that this was the testimony Jesus had given me from my convicted heart of prayer that Sunday morning in June.

During the various passages and seasons of trial, we give in to trying to think ahead of God. And what happens? We get on the wrong exit every time.

On December 2, 2001, the last prayer that Jesus had me to write down, He had begun to prepare me for the time of peaceful, rejuvenating sleep by blessing the Holy Spirit to have me ask Jesus Christ for His healing over an uncomfortable stitch that I had felt in my side and a feeling of a ball rolling around in my abdomen that had started early in the week. After prayer as usual I prepared my self for bed and the warring struggle of the night not knowing what darts, arrows or grips to expect but understanding that at my weakest point Jesus the Christ is strongest and all I had to do is just call on the mighty name of CHRIST JESUS *(Ps3:8)*. I awaken not to Satan's grip but to his announced presence in our home and intent. I felt a cold suffocating breeze over me. A noise that startled me to find that the house was pitch black; which was alarming because first of all there was no winter storm outside. Secondly we had night lights in the hallway, our daughter's room, and our bathroom for her comfort as she slept. So when I saw that all the lights were out I immediately jumped to my feet. Ran toward our daughters bedroom were she to had been awakened and had let out an ear piercing shriek. Frightened and trembling with fear she had buried her little face in her pillow screaming. I immediately grabbed her up covering her and shouted, "Not my child, but me! Jesus help us!" The Holy Spirit instructed me to move her toddler bed and take it in the room with my husband and me. So I went in and woke her father and asked him if he would please move her bed in our room in front of my closet where it stayed until January. That night my husband asked me why I felt our daughters' bed had to be moved in the room with us? I told him because the Holy Spirit instructed me to because Satan had badgered her in that instance and as terrified as she was, I was for her. So its best those at the most vulnerable hours of her little life, as she is sleeping and I'm in continual prayer until day break, it's safer for her to be under the anointed wing of shelter that God, Jesus Christ and the Holy Spirit has appointed in our home. And that is our bedroom. My husband never once looked at me as if I had really lost it, nor did he ever once complain about the tight inconvenience of having her little bed in our room along with our son's bassinette. He just hugged me and laid down putting his arms tightly and securely around me gently whispering, "It's going to be alright." Oh! I'm thankful to God for my designer husband! God knew what type of husband I needed and He created him just for me. And yes, I said it! God knew what type of husband I needed and not what kind of man I wanted, there is a difference. But we'll talk more about that at a later date.

# Dawn at Midnight

Matthew 9:22

There's nothing more exciting than a road trip especially when you leave at midnight traveling through the night into the next day. You really get to see God in majestic glory. To see the hues of the early morning sky as it blossoms into the fullness of morning from the chill of night with the energy of the sun dawning your face. There's nothing more exhilarating than being in the exuberant simplicity of our almighty creator God. During the peak of this voyage God blessed me to experience the freshness of the dawn of His early morning glory twice. The first time I remember feeling this was the morning that I woke realizing that Jesus blessed me to sleep undisturbed through the night, oh what a glorious morning that was. It was as if I had been placed in a bubble that was filled with calming energizing oxygen that just revitalized my total being. I was blessed to experience this restful sleep for two weeks, the last two weeks of the 2001 year. Prior to my two week rejuvenating peaceful sleep, God allowed me to have a dream and that was something I had not done for quite a while. In this dream my father had reinjured his back and was lying on the floor in his workshop with a continuous twitch and jerking motion barely able to respond to the questions that I was asking him. When he tried to respond his speech was very slurred and tears streamed from his eyes. I could see my mother, and my husband but I could only hear me asking my father, "Why didn't you just call for help before you tried to fix this yourself? Why didn't you just call Rod, *(my husband)*, and have him to come and do the heavy lifting for you? Now look what you've done to yourself, all you had to do was just ask for help!" Having awakened from that dream disturbed and confused I had made up my mind that I definitely wasn't going to ever share this with my mother, whom I'm very very close to. There's neither a morning that passes nor evening that we do not talk and share things as a mother and daughter should. But that would be one of very few things I decided not to share with my mother. I felt that I had to tell someone, so I had purposed to share it with my husband and never did because of the way that he worked. When he'd get in from work I would always be asleep or just very busy with our eighteen month old daughter and our two month old son, so there was never the opportune time when we were both awake or just leisure to talk about anything other than his day, diapers, feedings, and the latest episode of potty training. You would've thought I'd had it down to a science having potty trained lots of other children through out my fifteen years in my Early Childhood profession. Also during that time I was working feverously to make sure that my children, husband and immediate family had a memorable Christmas. Additionally I was completing letters I had begun in October to my husband, parents and sister as to what my wishes for my children would be in the event that something were to happen to me. You ask the question why? My answer I didn't understand why! But today I know that Jesus the Christ having walked this earth as a carnal man understood and empathized with the fact that I needed comfort in the security of knowing that I had expressed to my family my love for them and my children's well being. God knew that he needed my undivided attention, he needed all of my mind and heart clear and on one accord for what He had in store for me. God knew that I would need that rejuvenating energy and strength to be able to turn my face from the chill of night into the warm dawn of His glorious morning.

# Dawn of a New Day

Funny thing, the mind. God created the brain so that it would work similar to a sponge in water. It absorbs and retains our most fondest and painful memories and stores them into the deepest recesses of our mind. God allows the brain to hold those thoughts and memories there until He needs to use them in our life as encouragement, a guide, or reassurance. You remember I told you God had allowed me to experience the majestic glory of His sunrise at the peak of my exodus from my self, the chill of midnight, twice. Well the second time was when I was admitted into the hospital. That's right the hospital, it's like God switched cars on me in the middle of the trip. We got out of the Cadillac, a leisurely drive on the scenic route and jumped into a Porsche, on I-95 and mashed the accelerator to the floor. Destination, True Heart, Restoration.

It was New Years Eve morning 2002, a beautiful sunny crisp Sunday morning, awakening from another peaceful nights sleep, laying in bed thinking of my morning routine to prepare myself and family for church. I sat up and placed my feet on the floor and went into the bathroom. As I walked into the bathroom I noticed a feeling of pins sticking in the bottoms of my feet. I looked at the bottoms of my feet but there was nothing out of the ordinary in that moment. I continued with my routine and then looked down to began to lotion my feet when I noticed that they were strawberry red and it hurt to touch them. Walking was not a problem but I couldn't put on stockings or socks because it hurt to pull anything over them.

I did manage to put on a pair of booties. I mentioned it to my husband, but I really didn't think it was anything other than one of the many symptoms of Multiple Sclerosis (MS) that I had been diagnosed with in April 1994. I awakened on a Sunday morning completely blind in my left eye and partially blind in the right eye. This was the beginning of my journey of conviction unbeknownst to me. My reaction to this acute illness that attacked me one week after my twenty forth birthday, the purchase of my first convertible sports car and a promising career didn't affect me in a negative way. I was surprisingly positive and hopeful. I realize that my attitude during this crisis was an attitude that was totally touched by God. Why do I say that? On an ordinary day we may struggle with less severe issues, I'll go so far as to say, even petty interruptions, to disrupt our daily routine. And for many of us suddenly our attitudes are in the red, a negative charge! We allow the negativity that Satan begins to feed us to still our joy, peace, and hope for a brighter tomorrow. I felt this first hand daily while attending the neurological facility for my treatment. There were several other young adults with very promising careers that were experiencing the same acute crisis at that time but they were in a negative charge. They were having a very difficult time dealing with the interruption of there life so much so that they had very rotten attitudes towards those that were serving them. They were lost fumbling in the darkness unable to see the distant light of hope, and faith that Christ Jesus was going to work it out. Check the rear view mirror, God will really show you how far you've come on your journey, your exodus of self. All the while continually growing in faithful trust in Christ Jesus as He walks you through your exodus.

# Hues at Dawn

Moving forward in my journey, transitioning as the morning sky from dawn to sunrise, not knowing that the next phase of my exodus was at hand, I continued to press my way and I found some shoes to slide on that didn't hurt to terribly bad, helped my husband gather up the babies and off we went to church. I played for service just as usual, listened to the testimony service and the Church Mother that God chastised me for mimicking stood and thanked God for healing her of the Flu that she was just getting over from the past week. I immediately thought, I'm going to try to avoid her because getting sick with the Flu was the last thing I needed to do having two small babies. How would I take care of them when my husband left early hours of the morning for work and most of the time didn't return home until late evening. So church ended and in all my efforts to duck church mother, I didn't check my rear view mirror, she tapped me on the shoulder and called my name, "Tudyyyy!", all the while reaching up to give me a big hug and kiss on the cheek. I thought to my self, "GREAT!", just what I need a fifty percent chance of getting sick at a time that I really can't afford to because I had so much to do. After service my husband and I returned home, had dinner and put the kids down for a nap. Remember the pain and sensitivity in my feet? Well now, my entire body felt like I had been beat, and I was sore all over and had a headache that just wouldn't let up. I slept on the couch with my husband awaked feeling even worse, I was convinced that church mother had passed on the Flu virus to me. My husband stepped in and worked with the kids while I sat on the couch feeling as if I had run a marathon. As the night went on my condition continued to slowly worsen. In our family New Year's Day is a big feast day that's started out by taking down all the Christmas decorations and then we gather with, my family, my parents, my sister, any visiting family and friends and eat a big meal that always consists of a pot of beans with sides of fried chicken, fried fish, crabs, oysters, cakes and dad's sweet potato pie. But that New Year's Monday, I didn't move from the couch where I stayed in the same place all day long. I couldn't move because I had no strength to pick up my feet, what little I had I was using to take care of the babies that were right beside me on the couch. My husband was outside with the rest of the family taking down the Christmas decorations. As the day progressed my parents noticed that they hadn't seen me outside and asked my sister to walk over and see what I was doing. They were not aware that she had been over mid-morning to see the babies, and when she returned that late afternoon again she found me sitting in the same place that she found me earlier that morning. She put the bag that I had with the soiled pampers and pull-ups in them in the trash can, check the babies and went back outside to inform my mother that I was still in the same spot that I was this morning and that I had not put away any of the decoration that I had in the house. My mother realized that was odd for me not to be cleaning the house especially being cooped up in the house all day, so at the end of the day she came over to see what I had cooked and saw that I was just as my sister had described. She asked me how I was feeling, I told her not well, I had picked up the flu from the Church Mother and it was the worst flu I had ever experienced. My mother then offered to take the babies over to their home, but I assured her that with the help of my husband I could manage through the night. I felt that the worst of it was just about over, but little did I know the ride was just beginning. As I told you earlier mom and I always and still do today, talk before we turn in for the night. This time mom called to find the babies having a crying competition. She asked me "What in the world was going on with them?" I told her I didn't know because they were all dry and fed. Immediately she responded by telling me she and dad were coming to get the babies so I could rest. When mom and dad arrived and saw my declining condition, mom saw my struggle to gather the children's things for their over night bag. She felt my forehead to find that I had no fever but I felt clammy and cold, so she then proceeded to feel my back, arms, and legs they too were clammy and cold, the only warm spot on my body was around my heart. Dad asked me to call the doctor first thing the next morning and tell them I needed to come in because I had a very bad case of the flu. I did just that on Tuesday morning January 3, 2002. The doctor's office receptionist asked me if I could be there by 10:30 AM. I told them, Yes, I could. My husband was at home with me, he never left for work that morning because he said it just didn't feel right to leave me at home alone in my condition after watching and walking with me through the night from our bedroom to the couch in our den because I just couldn't find comfort in any position. There was no comfort laying down in the bed, laying on the couch, sitting on the couch, or even laying in my husbands arms as he assured me everything was going to be okay. I just couldn't find that comfort I was longing so desperately for. That "AHHH" moment in finding that just right spot. I called my mother, who had gone to work on my behalf that morning, to let her know that I had gotten an appointment for 10:30 that morning and that Rod was going to take me. After hanging up from talking with my mother I knew I needed to begin to get myself washed up and dressed for the doctor's appointment. At that point every breath that I took felt very lite and thin but I pressed my way onward down the hallway into our bedroom and into bathroom where I felt exhausted from the walk. I lite heartedly said to my husband, "Wow this flu is really kicking my butt!" He looked at me and smiled warmly and asked me what I wanted him to take out for me to wear. I told him that the way I felt, a sweat suit would make me look good. *You know when you were a kid and your mom took you to the doctor she always would tell you to put on your very best under wear, you know the ones that looked almost new. You only wore them when you stayed overnight with grandma or went to the doctors. My mom always reminded me of that from a child right up through my young adult years, and I do my kids the same way today.* About that time, *sound the alarm the Calvary had arrived,* my mom, *"need I say more!"* My mother gently said, "Oh no, you know these will not do" *(talking about the under garments),* and she began to bathe and dress me for the visit. I barely had stamina to brush my teeth or raise my arms to help dress myself.

I remember walking out the door of our home that morning never thinking that I would not be returning within a couple of hours. It was a twenty minute drive to Greenville, NC to my doctor's office, and my husband dropped mom and me at the front door so I wouldn't have far to walk. I walked in to the check-in desk but was too weak to give her my information so my mom did this for me. There were so many people in the waiting room that day I thought, "Oh I'll be here for a while." The air was getting thinner and my back was getting weaker. It had begun to be laborious to hold myself up in the position that relieved me the most that was leaning forward with my elbows propped on my knees. My husband held my hand because he didn't know anything else to do as my mom's warm hand gently massaged my back as she talked with my father on her cell phone. I continued to look towards the door in hopes of hearing my name called to see the doctor, getting medication I needed to feel better and returning home to my babies. Finally the nurse called my name and I walked through the door with every bit of strength I had left in me. As the door closed behind me, I fell to my knees. I had no strength left. The nurse and my mom caught me and put me in a wheel chair and wheeled me into a consultation room where I sat for a few moments and then the door opened, but it wasn't my doctor it was an intern on her first day. HOW IRONIC IS THAT! My mom asked where our family doctor was. The intern responded that he was seeing other patients and she would be working with me. I thought to myself, "It's just the flu how could she mess this up!" She proceeded by asking me questions about how I was feeling and I answered as best I could but I told her I was very weak. She didn't take a moments thought and said, "I'm going to start by sending you down to X-ray" and she had the nurse to wheel me straight there. As I sat there I talked with my mom saying to her that I didn't know much about medicine but in all my visits to the doctor the very next thing they'd do after they talk with you is to take your vital signs. I then asked mom if she remembered the intern taking my vitals because I didn't. She said," No she didn't take them, when we get back in the room we're going to ask for your doctor." Still in x-ray waiting and had been waiting for thirty minutes or longer I touched my mothers hand to get her attention and whispered to her that I can't hold myself up any longer I need to lay down. She informed the nurses at the desk and requested that a nurse wheel me back. In route to the consultation room the nurse informed my doctor's nurse of my condition. As I sat slumped in the wheel chair he entered the room and immediately realized that my heart was not functioning properly. He quickly grabbed the blood pressure cuff and began to get a blood pressure reading, but to his astonishment he couldn't get one. He tried once more and couldn't get a reading so he instructed his nurse to call EMS. He continued to search for a pulse and a heart beat but couldn't feel a pulse nor hear my heart beat. He calmly said to my mom, "Don't be alarmed, it's obvious her heart is beating or she wouldn't be talking, she wouldn't be alive." Mom looked at me and smiled warmly and said, "It's going to be alright, we'll meet you at the hospital." I assured her that I was okay and I'd be waiting for them. Christ Jesus had blessed me with an unspeakable calm within my spirit, as well as with the peaceful, warm assurance He had strengthened even more within my mother that permeated and began to lift me up (Psalms 91:11-12). As they wheeled me out on the stretcher I looked up and saw that it was snowing. I commented to the EMS workers that this was my most favorite time of the winter season because it's always so quiet when it snows and I always find refreshing comfort in the purity, and rejuvenation of life that takes place after a quite snow. They just smiled and continued to work feverously to prepare me for my grand entrance to the emergency room. That's right I said grand entrance because after getting processed and placed in a room, several doctors and nurses came in to see me. To disprove the EMS report that they had a lady who was still responsive and talking, but had no registering blood pressure, pulse or heart beat. Each one that entered took my vitals. I was thinking, "They just needed to turn the volume up on their stethoscopes for the heart beat." I didn't know what they needed to do for the blood pressure reading, but it had to be something as simple as faulty equipment, because I was still among the living! Praise the Lord! Ultimately, I knew Jesus Christ was in control. I had faith that He had appointed the physicians and nurses that were to care for me. God brought me to it! I knew He would bring me through it!

As I lay in the bed in growing discomfort with misery throughout my body I began to pray and ask God to heal the young lady that was in the cubical to the right of me. She kept screaming out in pain from the cramps that were attacking her body from her neck down to her toes. I think we've all experienced cramps in our legs or feet at some point so you understand the anguish and pain of a cramp. Now just imagine how she felt to have her entire body racked with that kind of pain. I remember hearing her cry so pitifully for someone to help her, but never calling on God. After praying for her relief, I then began to pray for God's intervention in my body because it seemed no one understood what was going on, but I knew He knew just what it was. He knew what they needed to do to get me up and on my way back home to my babies. See, I had faith in God's word that through Christ Jesus all things are possible. God allowed the Holy Spirit to flood my every thought with that scripture (*Mark 9:23 . . . All things are possible to him that believes . . .*). After having been in emergency for some time, at this point I'm still waiting to be seen by the doctor predestined to be mine, my parents at my bed side, and thinking of all my husband was doing at home to help my sister, and three Great Grandmothers get our children settled in at my parents home. I knew he was going to explain to our daughter where I was, because I told when she left with my parents that, "Mommy is going to all right, I promise!" The light came on for me that I needed to pray to Christ Jesus, my intercessor not only for my circumstance, but also for my husband, children and family. That He would wrap them in the feathers of His comfort, strength, and trust that it was and is through Him that all things were then and is today made possible. I'm thankful to God for allowing the Holy Spirit to bless me to not only hear Him, but understand Him and respond in a spirit of obedience to the knowledge He'd just blessed me with. Don't be mistaken. I knew how the scriptures read because I had been reading the scriptures since my youth as well as hearing the scriptures read and expounded on by the Elders. But that was the first time that I had heard it so crystal clear through the Holy Spirit that it literally warmed me from the inside. But still to anyone that touched me I was ice cold and clammy like a snake. My heart still not beating, just swinging very slowly was being incubated by Christ Jesus while He was waiting for my complete obedience. So I began to pray to Jesus the Christ reminding Him of God's word; like He needed reminding. I reminded myself, that all things were possible through Him, Christ Jesus, because it is He that was giving me the strength to speak and it was He that was sustaining me as I laid and prayed, so I asked Christ Jesus for His anointing and healing over my body and my heart. I asked Him to send me the doctor that God had predestined just for that season. And just as I finished that whispered prayer God sent the doctor in. The doctor addressed me and my parents and began to explain the understanding that had been given to him of what may have brought this on. He simply said it was a virus that attacked the heart muscle causing it to work twice as hard, exhausting it, causing fluid to build up in the sack around the heart. In short the heart was "drowning". He said they were going to move me, start me on medication to help relieve some of the fluid my body was now beginning to take on and run tests to see what procedures they would be performing. Hence the acceleration of my journey and my physical decline.

# Spectrum of Truth

As my body began to take on more and more fluid I began to swell and experienced increased pressure and pain in my back and between my shoulders felt like I was being stabbed over and over again. The nurses and my family continually adjusted my bed to try to keep me as comfortable as they possibly could as I was nearing the warmth of my sunrise. As I laid propped in my bed God allowed the Holy Spirit to bless me with a light of truth that warmed me so that as I began to share the insight of my journey to that point with my parents, of how on the first Sunday in June God had condemned my heart and I immediately asked for His forgiveness and prayed for a servants heart of conviction. I prayed for a testimony and He was answering that prayer, not the way I thought it would turn out, but the way God had already predestined it to be. He just needed for me to ask Him for it. Just as He tells in His word, *we have not because we ask not (Luke 11:9-10)*. My mother said that my skin brightened to the beautiful brown hue it was before and the more I shared with them the brighter the warm glow grew. At that instance she said she knew I had made it over and everything was indeed going to be alright. What was that light of truth? Pray with a pure heart: pray with your heart and mind as one. I shared that whispered prayer with my parents the conscious pray, and the evidence of the heart prayer that I was praying that had brought me to that highway marker of my journey *(Life)*. I expressed with urgency how important it was that we all take a moment before we pray to make sure that our hearts and minds are in sync because it is the prayers of the heart (*subconscious*) that our Lord and Savior Christ Jesus will intercede. While we're watching and waiting for an answer to the conscious prayers of our mind, or should I say mouth because we like to hear ourselves talk. Let me tell you that after that moment of truth my journey took a turn. Satan returned this time with even more gusto! Yes literally began to suffocate me. One of my nurses had just flushed and read the artery catheter in my neck so I wasn't to have it flushed and read again for thirty minutes. *(But my other nurse, who could really give a great sponge bath, but was slower than molasses on a cold winters day getting my readings because she was in training to learn how to take the readings, "HOW GREAT WAS THAT!" Returned and told me she needed to take another reading.") I expressed to her that it was getting more and more painful each time they laid me back to get that reading and she said, "I'll try my best not to keep you down to long."* As my bed reclined I began thinking of the small things that we all take for granted, such as a sitting up, raising your arms, bathing, and I began to express my thanks to her for the care that she took in serving me. Just as she was saying thank you, my bed had totally reclined, I began to feel myself being suffocated. I pulled myself up holding the rail of my bed and in my last conscious breathe, I called on my Savior Jesus the Christ as my body slumped saying, "Jesus, help me!" Immediately my parents were left in a moment of shock and surprise because I seemed to have been taking a turn for the better. Standing in the mist of what seemed to be tragic chaos, reflecting and collecting their thoughts of reasons as to what just happened? Not why, but what just happened? How do you respond, when it was all looking as if the sun had peaked, my journey had eclipsed into a yielding moment of still darkness. After being revived I felt a familiarity, a dejavu moment. I had already witnessed this moment in my life early on. In that moment of noise and hurried scuffle by the medical team to stablelize me, it was a time of quiet recollection for me. God allowed the Holy Spirit to whisper to me these words,

"It *wasn't your father, it was you.*" I immediately remembered the dream that I had of my father lying on his cold shop floor with a twitch and slurred speech and I was over joyed that it was indeed not my father. I began saying to each nurse and doctor that was trying to communicate with me that it wasn't him (my father), but it was me (the dream was intended for). The more I tried to express this I then realized that it *really* was me because my speech was slurred, no one could understand a thing I was saying and they were holding my upper body because I had a really bad twitch. As the twitch subsided my speech began to clear and they could understand what I was trying to say to them. One of the doctors looked me in the eyes and said as words of comfort and to keep me from being afraid I guess, "It's *going to be alright.*" I said, "*I know because it wasn't him, it was me, it was me.*" The doctor looked at me as if I were talking out of my head and proceeded to ask me if there was particular scripture I wanted read. I didn't know quite how to take that because that usually meant that you were on your way OUTTA HERE! So that meant that she didn't really believe that I was going to be OK! Now if I had been depending totally on her insight I would've really been over drawn on my Faith Account at First Faith Bank. But see my accounts had moved to Faith and Trust International Bank and my Personal Banker was at that time and is today Christ Jesus. He had already made my withdrawal. He knew what I needed and prepared my travelers checks for this leg of my journey. I'm thankful and blessed that He chose my account to oversee!

# In The Valley

Trusting in my God and remembering His instructions to me in His word, to find delight in the midst of trial (James 1:2-4, II Cor.12:10) and to be of good comfort, because my faith had made me whole (Matt.9:22), I asked the doctor to read me the 23 Psalms. I always found that to be a peaceful scripture. The doctor began to read and I began to thank God for my life and testimony, my conviction, sincerity of heart, and most importantly I thanked Him for choosing me as that witness of His grace, mercy, and deliverance out of myself into a convicted ambassador, that willing vessel. As the other doctors and nurses worked feverishly to assist in my stabilization the head cardiologist was informing me of the next series of attempted procedures to be done. I agreed and set my attention back on Jesus's quite reassuring comfort, *"You're going to be alright."* That comfort warmed me internally so that I couldn't feel the extreme cold of the prep room or the pain from all that they were sticking in my arms and legs to prepare me for the procedure. As I lay there waiting I began to sing the song *"Jesus, Oh What A Wonderful Child"* to myself. The song was another blanket of comfort that cradled me like an infant in the arms of its parents. Like that old spiritual humming that grandma does, like no other, to quiet and comfort the restless little one, it warms them and lets them know everything is going to be alright. During this process of preperation there was one doctor that kept walking over to me to reassure me and to help me breathe and each time that he would come over he would say, "look into my eyes" and I would smile because

God had blessed him with really beautiful bright, warm, caring eyes that God used as a confirming vessel of comfort. The last time he walked over, before he could say anything I told him I was tired and I was ready to get some rest. He smiled and told me, "Okay, it's time. Breathe in deep as you can and look into my eyes." I said, "Thank you Jesus", and did just as he instructed. As I looked into his eyes that last time I felt another internal warmth and closeness to Jesus and my heavenly Father, God. I began to hear a soft sound that comforted me like nothing I had ever heard before. *"I know you think it was the pain medication working!"* But it wasn't, because I heard this beautiful sound the entire three and a half weeks that God had me at rest. It was a beautiful melody of brilliance, like the sun rising just over the morning horizon. Gentle warming strength, like the warmth of the Fall sun on your face at mid-day. This beautiful gift of comfort crescendo into a strong refreshing brilliance of newness that we occasionally experience when you see God's brilliance in a beautiful rainbow just after a late evening rain shower. Just before the sun begins its descent into a magnificent sun set. (*Close your eyes, inhale slowly. Now exhale . . . . Feel God's renewing.*) That tingling warmth that you experince in that few minutes of God's awsome power that He allows us to experience when we take the time to bask in the Grace of His Magnificance is what I felt and what sustained me. And just as I try to describe that feeling of His merciful awesomeness and grace, close your eyes and imagine yourself sitting in front of a symphony orchestra listening to the beautiful sounds of each instrument separately and then collectively as they began to play very softly gradually building on the swell of sound until the peak of brilliance of that arrangement is peaked into that crescendo! It gives you chills. That's just how God orchestrated the events of my rest during that three and a half week period of mines and my family's life while the doctor's had me on life support. God had me cradled in the comfort of Jesus the Christ, my Lord and Savior. There was no doubt I knew that He was with me and what God willed was going to be alright. I was going to be alright! My family was going to be alright! My husband and children were going to be alright! I knew this because I asked God to strengthen and bless us all early on before this event that I had come to understand that God already had planned and conditioned me for. In realizing that God planned it, in the midst of this trial, I realized that He'd already prepared me for this journey. God had already packed me, planned the trip and made my reservations. The only thing I had to do to confirm my reservation was to trust, and believe that Christ Jesus was my intercessor and that God's will would be done. And in believing in Jesus in my last breath, I was blessed with the strength to call on the wonderful name of Jesus at my weakest moment, and in that instance God poured out His warm loving grace and mercy over me. That's why out of a team of six doctors none of them could understand the origin of my sudden illness. Why I was cold every where except over my heart, a heart that wasn't beating on it's own but with a ventalater. Why at one point midway the second week of being on the vent my other organs started to fail at which time one of the physicians (*set by the enemy, Satan, to cast a spirit of distrust and hopelessness in Christ Jesus*) told my family that the only way that I would be going home would be after a heart transplant or in a body bag because all of the other organs had begun to fail. Now you're may be asking yourself what was so bad about the heart transplant. Nothing, it was just that the transplant list is overwhelmingly long. After the physician made that statement and then put me on the heart transplant list, my name was moved to the top of the list, first priority. See how God works! There have been some people on the list for two or more years. They couldn't understand how that happened. That mustard seed of faith that God speaks about in (Luke 17:6), he not only strengthen in me but also in my parents and husband. They enlightened the doctors that in all things God has the last say and through and by the strength and power of Jesus the Christ all things are possible. As I lay there

God had continued to work in me and in my family. He answered my journaled prayers in which I had asked Him to strengthen my family even more so that we could continue to work in the ministry with my father, who God had called and ordained when I was child around the age of eight. I asked God to strengthen my father's ministry and show my mother the gift or gifts in the ministry that He had blessed her with. I also asked Him to strengthen and anoint my husband to be the Godly man that He would have him to be. Those powerful words of faith and claimed deliverance were spoken over me as I lay there as a witness to any non-believers present at that pre-ordained time to soften the ground in preperation for the seed to be planted. Never the less, I understand that the unbelieving doctor walked away shaking his head with an expression of disbelief. *Disbelief in the power of God the creator of all things. The author of all knowledge and understanding that's given to each and everyone of us as believers or non believers for His divine and pre-ordained purpose.* As my prognosis and vitals continued to decline my parents sat by my bedside and continued to pray. My husband returned home to spend time with the children and take care of some business that I would normally handle. He prayed to God every step of the way for increased strength in this unexpected exit of his journey, as God was allowing him to be propelled into true independent faith and parenthood. Being faced with walking the journey of parenthood without me, by mans prognosis. But by knowledge of Gods word and promises, my husband was able to stand with what seemed to be spiritually wobbly legs of faith, to his ever strengthening spiritual feet of faith. Unknowingly to me at that time, but became evident to me in the weeks and months following, God had already begun to plant my husband firmly in the spiritual landscape of His kingdom. See, my husband and I during that time would talk about any and everything, but he'd always go mute when we would begin to talk about how his relationship and walk with God the Father and His son, our intercessor, Jesus the Christ.

He'd static out like the am/fm radio stations do as you travel from your home town into a different city and state. So you can only imagine what a wonderful gift that realization was to me. But what put me in awe the most is that God had touched the community of believers in my home town to stop at noon and have unified prayer for me and my family. Now if that isn't some indescribable power and movement of God's Holy Spirit, I don't know what is! God used me and my family as a catalyst of prayer and of unity in Christ for those that believed and as a light and example to the lost and unbelieving in our community of Washington, North Carolina as well as to those in our presence in Chapel Hill, N.C. Isn't God awesome!!

He just wants us to stop and let go of the map, the steering wheel, and the shovel that we use to fill our pot holes of life along the way. Let God, Jesus the Christ and His ever present Holy Spirit be the map maker, navigational team, and highway construction team of our journey, *journey of life*. That's just what my family and I have done. I LET GO! THEY LET GO! AND LET GOD HAVE HIS WAY! And because we did, God was able to full fill my *reservations*. I was able to take refuge and rest in the renewing of His comforting peace.

# Day Before Sunrise

Jesus had sent His legion of angels to deliver me from the grip of Satan. My parents witnessed that deliverance in my hospital room at UNC Chapel Hill the night before the morning of my next sunrise. The day God raised me up!

As my parents sat at my bed side until the last possible minute of hospital visitation unknowingly, on the night before my dawn of restoration, Jesus sent His angels through my room window. They entered into my room as three blue lights that circled my bed. One rested at my head and the other two, one at each foot. My parents looked at each other and wouldn't speak of what they witnessed with each other. Because as Satan uses our weakest moment as opportunity to knock us breathless, for a brief moment my mom said they automatically thought of what the older generation of their childhood traditionally would have said, those were the death angels. She said they immediately began to pray and God allowed the Holy Spirit to encourage her to read Psalm 91 again. She did and immediately shared the scripture with my father, which reassured and strengthen their faith even more. My parents left the hospital that night with a renewed faith in God's healing and deliverance. Now remember, one of my prayers that I journaled was for God to strengthen the ministry of my father and my mother. Well if God hadn't allowed me the opportunity to enter into this season of my journey, then my mom would not have been able to receive the revelation of her ordained blessing that God had been using her in for years, unknowingly to her, with the sick whose path she was blessed encounter and was an encouragement to. Mom shared with me that later on that night as she slept that God allowed the Holy Spirit to begin showing her all those sick individuals that she had served in the past through prayer and a soothing caressing touch. He just showed her caressing their shoulder or back and she said there was a glow around her hands. The Holy Spirit then showed her rubbing my abdomen and massaging my feet and the glow was around her hands. She said she sat up in the bed because she thought she was dreaming because it was like a movie was playing only she was awake. She looked down at her hands and she said that same glow that she saw around me before I entered my rest, the same glow the Holy Spirit revealed to her that night in the vision, that same glow was around her hands. She awakened my dad and began to share with him again what the Holy Spirit had showed her and in amazement said, "Why would God choose me to use as a vessel of healing hands? Little ole me! I can't believe it!" In awe of the revelation of God's magnificent, she opened her heart even more to serve as a willing vessel doing what ever the Lord allowed the Holy Spirit to give her to do. Always working in obedience to God the Father (Ecclesiastes. 9:10, I Corinthians 15 :).

# Angel Eyes

There's nothing like being awake to see the sun rise. Not getting up as the sun rises! But up with a nice cup of hot tea, a warm sweater on, and standing outside looking towards the rising sun. Feeling the warmth of Gods hand on your face as you turn your cheek to meet Him in all His glory in the rising of His creation, the sun. Ahhh! Peace . . . . Comfort . . . . Thankfulness . . . . Praise . . . . Refreshed . . . . Renewed . . . . Revived. That's how I felt at God's awakening on January 25, 2002, three days after having been taken off the ventilator that was helping to sustain me for three and a half weeks. He awakened me with a warming beautiful brilliance of indescribable angelic, heavenly orchestra of music. Music that I heard only on one other occasion during my five and a half year recovery. And on that occasion God allowed the Holy Spirit to show me the next leg of my journey pre-ordained by Him and for the glory of His kingdom. WOW! That's a testimony for another day!

When my heavenly Father woke me, my eyes focused in on my CD player that my husband and parents brought to the hospital for me to have when I woke from my pre-ordained passage of restoration. And don't you know Satan was immediately on the job once again trying to have me think that the music I heard was from the CD player, but Jesus was right there lighting the way. I asked my parents, who were there at that time,
"Why did you cut off the beautiful music?" My mother answered back," We haven't been playing any music." I said, "You're kidding." Mom assured me that they hadn't, because

I was in critical care, and they were given strict instructions not to talk above a whisper, play the TV above level set by the nurse, which was low enough for the mice to hear, or make any sudden loud outburst. So there was no way that they were playing the CD player as loud as I said the music was. They hadn't played the radio at all. I took in what they said, looked around the room and said," I thought the walls were different?" My parents then shared with me that I had been transported by helicopter from Pitt Memorial Hospital, and was now in UNC Chapel Hill Cardiac Medical Center. I looked at them with a smile and said, "Wow I missed the second helicopter ride of my life. Do you think I could get that Jello and Apple Juice I asked for yesterday?" That's when Dad said, "It's not yesterday baby, but three and a half weeks later, Jan. 25, 2002, 9:00A.M. Do you remember that the doctors at the referring hospital told you they were going to "freeze your brain", put you in an induced comma so you wouldn't remember any of the pain and trauma you had gone through?" I said, "yes, but I do remember . . . . I remember a lot of the details before they put me out and while I was out of commission, napping." Then I thought . . . that brain freezing business is really serious, I've lost a lot of time. "Oh well that was then, I'M BACK NOW, FEEL'N BETTER THAN EVER! No wonder I'm hungry." My father called the nurse and she notified the team of doctors. They came in immediately to see what was going on. Immediately they began to try to formulate a medical hypothesis as to how and why the sudden recovery of a patient that they had projected would have less than a twenty percent chance of surviving, without a heart transplant as soon as possible, was sitting up talking, smiling, and ready to eat so I could get back home to my babies.

As each doctor began to ask me questions to begin assessing my capabilities both cognitively and motor, I immediately recognized a familiarity about one of the doctors. Mind you, I had never laid eyes on him before in my life, until that day, but

I knew that I had seen those eyes before. They were the last eyes that I looked into before entering into the rest that God had in store for me with my Lord and Savior cradling me in the comfort of His feathers (Ps. 91:1-18). As God assures us in His word that Jesus would give His angels charge over us, I know that He did just that before the procedure began in the operating room at Pitt Memorial. One of His angels was there present with me. I know this because before the angel who appeared to be a man, a very handsome man with gorgeous eyes, would always start his statement of assurance with, "Look into my eyes, you're going to be fine. Look into my eyes . . . . you're doing great, I'm going to give you some oxygen . . . . just a little longer." I had been working hard, panting to breathe for quite some time as my condition was seemingly deteriorating, I began to explain to him that I was tired and just wanted to rest. He smiled and said, "Look into my eyes" and then asked me, "What's that song that you're humming?" I said, "Jesus, Oh What a wonderful Child", it was the song that I played in church New Years Eve Sunday. He said," That's a beautiful song." This gentleman, who Jesus had in place as one of the Pitt Cardiac medical team, confirmed with a beautiful smile that warmed me from the inside out, the blanket of comforting trust and unquestionable faith that I had. I knew I was in the care of my Lord and Savior Jesus the Christ. And following that smile, again he said, "Look into my eyes, it's time. Breathe and look into my eyes." I commented with my last conscious breath, "You have beautiful eyes." It was just something about those eyes. They were heavenly.

So to my awe, when the lead cardiologist walked into my room, there was a familiarity about him. I immediately said to him, I've seen you somewhere. He smiled and I immediately recognized those eyes. There they were. The heavenly eyes of one of my angels.

# Visitor's Center

It surprised one doctor on the team to the point of offense that I was so mentally coherent, verbal and truthfully responsive that I didn't see him any more after my first day of being conscious and back among the living. That particular doctor kept saying, "I don't understand how it is that you're able to do what your doing, because scientifically your not suppose to even be living, much less doing all that your doing." I looked him directly in his eyes and said," I'm here because God has me here. He has me here as a witness to and for you and all others that Jesus Christ blesses my path to cross." That doctor looked at me, red in the face, turned and walked out of my room and I didn't see him any more from that day to the day I was released, some two weeks later. The other doctors on the team began to tell me that I most likely wouldn't be able to walk without going through extensive physical therapy because of having been on life support for so long. They told me having been on the ventilator for three and a half weeks, it was possible my nervous system could have sustained damage that may have left me unable to walk. They began testing my nerve sensation and reflexes at the bottom of my feet. God had restored my feeling and reflexes in both my feet and legs. They then proceeded to test my arms and hands of which I did have feeling in both, but God had not yet ordained that I should have use of my hands and fingers just yet. He had another humbling horizon for me to reach. You know, we all take the privilege of the ability to use our hands, and limbs for granted. As well as all the other amenities to this temporary temple that God has given us to vacation in until He calls us to rest or His imminent return, which ever is first. Because we're so busy being busy, we forget to stop and be *"GRATEFUL."* To give God reverent thanks for the awesomeness of mobility and the way that He has hard wired us to be able to move each limb independently of the other, create expression on our faces, think, process and speak! We forget about the privilege of ability. The ability to be about what God created us for. **HIS GLORY! THANKFULNESS! PRAISE! WORSHIP!**

# HUMBLE SOUP

The doctors approved a dietary plan for me and I was able to have a meal of soup, and solid foods, no salt. Oh wow! You talk'n about being excited to eat. I was like a kid waiting to eat a slice of pizza. When my tray arrived, I got all propped up in the bed with a little help. To be expected! My parents got my tray positioned and my food and utensils layed out. I confidently reached for my spoon so I could begin to eat my soup when I realized my hand was over the spoon but my fingers weren't bending. My Mom gently took my hand, softly saying," let me help you." Wow, that is humbling . . . . I thought! You know the saying, "What goes up, must come down." It's the same with, "what goes in must come out!" Ha! I can laugh about it now. Well let me tell you my ego had a head on collision at the intersection of daily living skills and pride. What life was and the reality of life for me at that very moment. Not only could I not feed myself, but I couldn't go to the bathroom without help. To add insult to injury, I had to use a bed side commode. You're probably thinking that's not so bad. It is when it's not the most pleasant one of the two digestive elimination processes and your parent's have to clean you for the first time since you were potty trained. Now, what's humbling? It brought me to tears as I rested on my father's shoulder as he helped to support me while my mother cleaned me, because I didn't have the use of my hands nor strength, only desire. Whoo! It was so humbling for me that I had to pray to Christ Jesus and asked him to help me express my gratitude to my parents. It was important to me that they knew I didn't take what they did to help me for granted. It wasn't a big deal for them, but it was an emotional struggle within me, I wanted them to know how grateful I was.

You see, God already knew that I needed a humbling of my otherwise unnoticed prideful heart, to get me to the next destination, one of genuine heart felt gratefullness. That's a thanks that can't be contained, it fills your inner most being, your spirit. A thanks of urgency that you are compelled to express to someone with the ordained awareness, your eyes wide open to see how God has and is working in your life. One of reverent gratefulness to God and Jesus Christ for that person or circumstance that brought you to that point of humbling gratefulness and glorifying praise. On the afternoon of January 25th God allowed the Holy Spirit to begin to teach me how to give Him glory and praises of thanks in every part of my life and daily activities (Proverbs 3:5-6). It's easy to take life as you know it, or the helps that you're afforded for granted.

Okay so now you're thinking she's one of *those people,* fanatical! Your right, I Am! Fanatical in my DESIRE (Psalms 119:10) to walk in constant awarness and gratefulness of, and to, God the Father and my Lord and Savior Jesus the Christ, so that I am WILLFULLY ( Psalms 40:8, Proverbs 8:34) doing what He created me to do in every aspect of my life. Which is to worship God giving him all the glory, honor, praise of thanksgiving, and gratefulness with conviction. Understand that to be thankful is to acknowledge a gift of blessing. Gratefulness is cherishing with the full awareness that it is because of God and the intercessions of Jesus Christ that you "ARE!" And being in awe of Gods love, grace, mercy and guidance of His Holy Spirit in every second of our lives. Living life without regret but in reverence of the awesomeness of God and our Lord and Savior Jesus Christ.

Take a minute and look back at the three words that are capitalized. Wondering why? Desire is a very necessary character trait, gift from Jesus that we must have to stay the course, to become experienced travelers of the voyages that God allows us to take. Voyages that He pre-ordained for us at our unformed creation (1 Corinthians 10:13, Psalms 139: 1-6, 13-17). Another reason we want desire and not determination alone is because you are coming into the full awareness of a genuine love from your heart for Jesus realizing that YOU would not BE if it weren't for Jesus revealing you to the Father so that He would choose you and begin to allow the Holy Spirit to bless you with truth, understanding and wisdom. With the blessing of Godly desire you have an ever deepening yearning to be in His presence, to have a relationship with Jesus that allows you to glorify the Father with every fiber of your being. And that yearning propels your determination to do the will of God. To do what's right, to practice righteousness in our daily passage of life as often as humanly possible (Philippians 1:10-11, 4:13). And let's not forget with desire comes promise, (Psalms 37:4). (*Journal thoughts, reflections, prayers or notes*)

_____

_____

_____

_____

_____

_____

_____

_____

_____

_____

_____

_____

_____

In the beginning of my recovery God allowed the Holy Spirit to strengthen and continually encourage me throughout my voyage of rehabilitation with scriptures of encouragement and affirmation. Even still today as I travel the passage that God allows and again has pre-ordained as a blessing for me and those whose paths I cross directly or indirectly, He allows the Holy Spirit to keep me encouraged and affirmed in my voyage with these scriptures among others. As the Holy Spirit ushers me through a spiritually guided crossing of meditation and reflection, I am reassured and strengthened in the consciousness of the reconstruction of deliverance in my life that I couldn't have ever navigated through without Jesus Christ and God's Holy Spirit in my life.

Take a moment to reflect how God has worked in your life by reading, and meditating on each of these scriptures. I've found that writing out your thoughts, prayers and praises of gratefulness is a very important key action that can help enhance your passage of spiritual, emotional and physical healing and rehabilitation.

Lamentation 3:25 _____

_____

_____

_____

_____

_____

_____

_____

_____

_____

_____

_____

_____

_____

Isaiah 40:31 _____

_____
_____
_____
_____
_____
_____
_____
_____
_____
_____
_____
_____
_____
_____
_____
_____
_____
_____
_____
_____
_____
_____
_____
_____
_____
_____
_____
_____
_____
_____
_____
_____
_____

Jeremiah 29:13 _____

_____

_____

_____

_____

_____

_____

_____

_____

_____

_____

_____

_____

_____

_____

_____

_____

_____

_____

_____

_____

_____

_____

_____

_____

_____

_____

_____

_____

_____

_____

_____

Proverbs 2:3-5 _____

_____
_____
_____
_____
_____
_____
_____
_____
_____
_____
_____
_____
_____
_____
_____
_____
_____
_____
_____
_____
_____
_____
_____
_____
_____
_____
_____
_____
_____
_____
_____
_____
_____

Psalms 119:2, 20, 40 _____

Psalms 94:19

Roman 12:1-2 _____

Psalms 69:32 _____

_____
_____
_____
_____
_____
_____
_____
_____
_____
_____
_____
_____
_____
_____
_____
_____
_____
_____
_____
_____
_____
_____
_____
_____
_____
_____
_____
_____
_____
_____
_____
_____
_____
_____
_____

# Willful Passage

I stated that I wanted to willfully, *"intentionally, voluntarily"*, do what it is that God created me to do. Being human, we willfully do something to satisfy our own desires. Most of the time we attend events or participate in activities out of tradition without regard to how and why it started or just out of a desire to appease family, and friends. Willfully seeking the approval and acceptance of those around us. How many times in a day can you, will you consciously account for that same willful desire to glorify God in everything, every decision of your day? Walking actively in God's word which is His stamp of approval (James 2:14). God tells us to seek first the kingdom of heaven (Matthew 6:33), thereby seeking first His approval, not the group. Understand that walking in the obedience of His word will come a blessing of promise. A promise that He, God the Almighty, will add all other things unto us. Not man. El Shaddai, all sufficient, blesses us with favor in the eyes of family, friends and our enemies. And through all circumstances of our lives. Genesis 50:20, "What the enemy meant for harm, God intended for good to accomplish what is now being done, the saving of many lives." Through your witness of His blessings of perseverance, faith, and deliverance you become a willful vessel. A vessel that He uses to bless, encourage and shine a light that draws those that God intends to cross your path closer to Christ Jesus. And molds and strengthens even more your faith, love and obedience to Christ Jesus our Lord and Savior.

Take a moment to reflect and record how often you remember willfully purposing everything about your day to the glory of God, willfully walking in His approval? Not focusing on whether or not you fell off the wagon of success in completing your goal. Daily life is like an off road adventure, you never know what kind of terrain is ahead. As hard as we try we may miss a turn or run up on hilly, rocky passages more often than we expect to or care to remember. But reflect on your intent and desire for God's approval in your daily life verses seeking the daily approval of family, friends, or the popular clique. Then pray to the Father in the name of his son Jesus the Christ to give you the daily strength you need and desire to walk willfully designing everything about your day to the glory of God and Jesus Christ. Keeping in mind we're not perfect, we now have to incorporate the intentional action of thought before action or reaction with our prayer of faith and watch how God works. Pray to the Father in the name of his son Jesus Christ to allow the Holy Spirit to minister to you and to guide you in your daily passage of willful praise and glory to Him. SHHHH . . . . BE STILL. SHHHH . . . BE QUITE. WAIT! Wait on the Lord Psalms 31:24. (*Reflect, Pray, Meditate, Praise*)

---
---
---
---
---
---
---
---
---
---

What did God create us to do? To fear Only Him (1 Samuel 12:24, Deuteronomy 10: 12-13, 2 Timothy 3:16-17). Give Him glory, honor, and praise. (Psalms 100:1-5, 136:1-26,

Hebrew 13:15). To bring to light for everyone what His plan is (Ephesians 3:9-10, Hebrews 2:12). How can we do that? By being a living, walking witness of willful obedience. Through that obedience we are giving God and Jesus Christ the glory. In our society we learn at an early age to care about what others think of us or precieve us to be. Sometimes we get so wrapped up in what others think of us, we loose ourselves and loose site of God's pre-ordained plan for our lives. We're trapped in a tornado of human compliance! Traditional compliance! What follows? Emotional tragedy, bewilderment, misunderstanding and confusion and a disconnected relationship with God and Jesus Christ. What happened to Godly compliance in our busy, so we think, all important self driven lives? We get so self driven that we affirm daily within ourselves if I don't do it for me, who will? Or if I don't look out for me, then who will? We're so self absorbed we forget JESUS has sustained us. In our travels with Jesus we are V.I.P, (Very *Important People with a Very Important Privilege)* not sometimes but all of the time. He clears our pathway so there isn't any misunderstanding or confusion. Only clarity of life and direction through truth and obedience of His expectations clearly stated in His written word, the BIBLE and exemplified in His living word as it applies to our daily lives (James 1:22). To have a blessed life is to live to the glory of God. To live to God's glory is to be obedient actively living in His word. To actively live in God's word we have to become willfully desiring vessels of God's righteousness not self righteousness.

# The Scenic Route

Today we have all these wonderful new bypasses that we can take when we travel to save time by going little country towns, two lane roads, and the busy little business areas that we run into when we travel from city to city. Well, let me tell you, Jesus took me on the scenic route during my recovery. I went through every country town, two lane road, dirt and paved, running into all types of weather, finding myself stuck for periods of time. I went to every busy little city getting held up in traffic jams that seemed to last forever. My friends, I'm talking about the physical, mental, emotional, and financial struggles Jesus allowed me to go through during my time of what I thought was going to be a quick and speedy recovery. I found out that God had more major adjustments to do in this vessel in whom He had just performed a spiritual heart transplant. Just as after a physical heart transplant your body has to go through a period of acceptance of the new heart. It has to build up an immune system while not rejecting the donor heart. You have to go through a cardiac rehabilitation. Learn the healthy way to eat, manage stress and your weight. Once you've successfully completed all the levels of the program the medical staff gives you a certificate and a scrapbook of your accomplishments while you attended the program, wishes you well and sends you on your way. Well it's the same way with a spiritual heart transplant with one major difference. Jesus is doing the heart rehabilitation training, and His program never ends nor does He ever leave you (Deuteronomy 31:6, Hebrew 13:5).

When God raised me up on January 25, 2002, I knew then when He blessed my eyes to open I had accepted His commission to be a faithful witness of His power, grace, and mercy. I was to tell the world. I just didn't know how. At first I thought I was to write a series of songs, but there was no way I was going to be able to tell how God had delivered me through song. Then I thought, "Lord people are going to get tired of hearing the same testimony over and over again, but if that's what I'm to use to fulfill my commission then help me do it in a way that's going to make You shine, that's going to glorify You." So I began my commission in the hospital that very day, January 25th.

That witness spilled over to the group that God had blessed me to be in cardiac rehab with, family members, friends, employees, doctors, nurses, the bill collectors on the phone, even to myself. I found that I was witnessing everyday in some way to anyone that Jesus put in my path. I had no idea that God had ordered my voyage to write a book. LOL! Me! An author! Ha! I hadn't accomplished anything that was book worthy! One day as I sat in quiet meditation God allowed the Holy Spirit to answer my ramblings, "Your right YOU haven't but Jesus has." You know how you feel when you have a dizzy spell? That was me at that very moment. The Father had spoken and I was to move forward in obedience. Not asking how, or why? But WHAT? What do you want me to do? What do you want me to say? What do you want me to write? God allowed the Holy Spirit to keep me encouraged by ministering and witnessing to me at my lowest times of God's three miraculous healings in my life. The first being the restoration of my sight after having gone blind at the age of twenty four for three months. My second season of healing came some four to five years after I was diagnosed with Multiple Sclerosis at the age of twenty six. Jesus Christ and God's Holy Spirit ushered me once again through a third season of healing. Jesus the Christ blessed me with His grace and mercy making even more evident to me God's healing and restoration of both my spiritual being and my physical body. During these seasons God allowed the Holy Spirit to continually minister to me bringing back to memory God's scriptures of promise which encouraged me both spiritually and physically to continue on in unwavering faith and trust. The Holy Spirit kept me encouraged to speak life and to continue to press my way, not just in word in action! Walking into my blessing of deliverance and healing even when the enemy was trying to feed my mind with doubt causing the body to weaken in response to the mind. I called on Jesus from whence cometh my help Psalms 121:2-8. I didn't pray and then focused on the negative circumstance. I didn't pray asking Jesus Christ to restore me and then continued to claim the illness. I prayed believing! I prayed receiving! I prayed claiming! Then I walked in my deliverance and healing!

I then began to worry less about how we were going to be able to pay for my heart medications, food, the mortgage, car payments, utilities, the basic necessities in life, and the consolidation of credit card bills we had accumulated debt on when we built our home and started my husbands' new business. Now add to that all the outstanding medical bills that insurance wouldn't cover. We were suddenly in more debt than we could have ever imagined. But you know what? Jesus brought us to it and He walked us through it! PRAISE GOD! Not only did Jesus use that passage as a booster shot of faith, but as a journey of naked truth. Naked truth is not dressed up with leaves of pride. Jesus stripped both our leaves of pride down to new born humility and truth. No longer was I just being a witness to how God restored my life, shining half the light in the vessel. But I was willfully desiring and allowing Jesus to use me, the vessel I prayed to be, to full capacity, shining the full reflection of light from the silver He was refining in me ( Psalms 66:10-14). Witnessing to the humbling truth of what God has, was, and is doing in my life.

What are some refining seasons *(trials)* God has allowed in your life? How were you strengthened *(refined)*?

# Pressing Toward The Horizon

I am so grateful to Jesus that He loved me enough to show me to the Father on the first Sunday in June 2001, the beginning of desired passage. Because of His grace I could begin my passage in becoming a vessel that God allowed to enter into the refining process. A process that would allow me to begin to be navigated and used in the way that God had pre-ordained. It is truly a blessing to be chosen to walk with Jesus Christ, doing the will of God the way He wants me to, and when He wants me to. I pray God's continued strength as I willfully continue this journey with Jesus the Christ. *"Not that I have already obtained all this, or have already arrived at my goal, but I press on to take hold of that for which Christ Jesus took hold of me. Brothers I do not consider myself yet to have taken hold of it. But one thing I do: Forgetting what is behind and straining toward what is ahead, I press on toward the goal to win the prize for which God has called me heavenward in Christ Jesus." (Philippians 3:12-14, NIV)*

My friends, be encouraged that no matter your circumstance pray believing that Jesus has already packed your bags with the necessary armor needed to make this journey. Pray receiving with open arms the blessings of God's timely deliverance. Pray claiming your blessings and the strength of Christ Jesus to carry you. Now trust and walk in that strength and faith! You're already packed! JESUS BROUGHT YOU TO IT! HE'LL BRING YOU THROUGH IT!

I am Tuyet Beatty-Moore, a Christian. A willful vessel to and for the glory of God!